A Gift for Fran

By Clem King

It is Fran's big day.

"Fran likes buns," said Mish.
"Buns can be her gift."

"Sift this so the buns
will be soft!" said Sten.

"Look! It sifts well!" said Mish.

"Can you get the milk, Mish?"
said Sten.

"We have no milk left!"
said Mish.

"Let's dash to the shop then!" said Sten.

"Mum, can we get a lift to the shop?" said Mish.

They got back home
with the milk.

"I will lift the milk, and Mish
can mix it in," said Sten.

"Do not spill it!" said Mum.

"Fran, this gift is for you!"
said Mish.

"Yum!" said Fran.

"The buns are so soft!"

CHECKING FOR MEANING

1. What did Mish think would be a good gift for Fran? *(Literal)*

2. How did Sten and Mish get milk for the buns? *(Literal)*

3. How do you know Fran liked the buns? *(Inferential)*

EXTENDING VOCABULARY

gift	Look at the word *gift*. How many sounds can you hear? What is another word that has a similar meaning? E.g. present.
sift	What does the word *sift* mean? What does sifting do to the flour that is used to make the buns? What kitchen equipment can you use to sift?
left	What are some different meanings of the word *left*? Use it in some sentences to show its different meanings, e.g. *I write with my left hand. I left my bag on the bus.*

MOVING BEYOND THE TEXT

1. What do you like to cook? Who helps you to cook?

2. Besides cakes or cookies, what else have you given someone as a birthday gift? E.g. clothes, flowers, a book to read.

3. What are other occasions when you give someone a gift?

4. Why do people like receiving gifts that have been made at home?

SPEED SOUNDS

ft	mp	nd	nk	st

PRACTICE WORDS

Sift

gift

soft

sifts

left

lift

and

sift